THIS COLORING BOOK BELONGS TO:

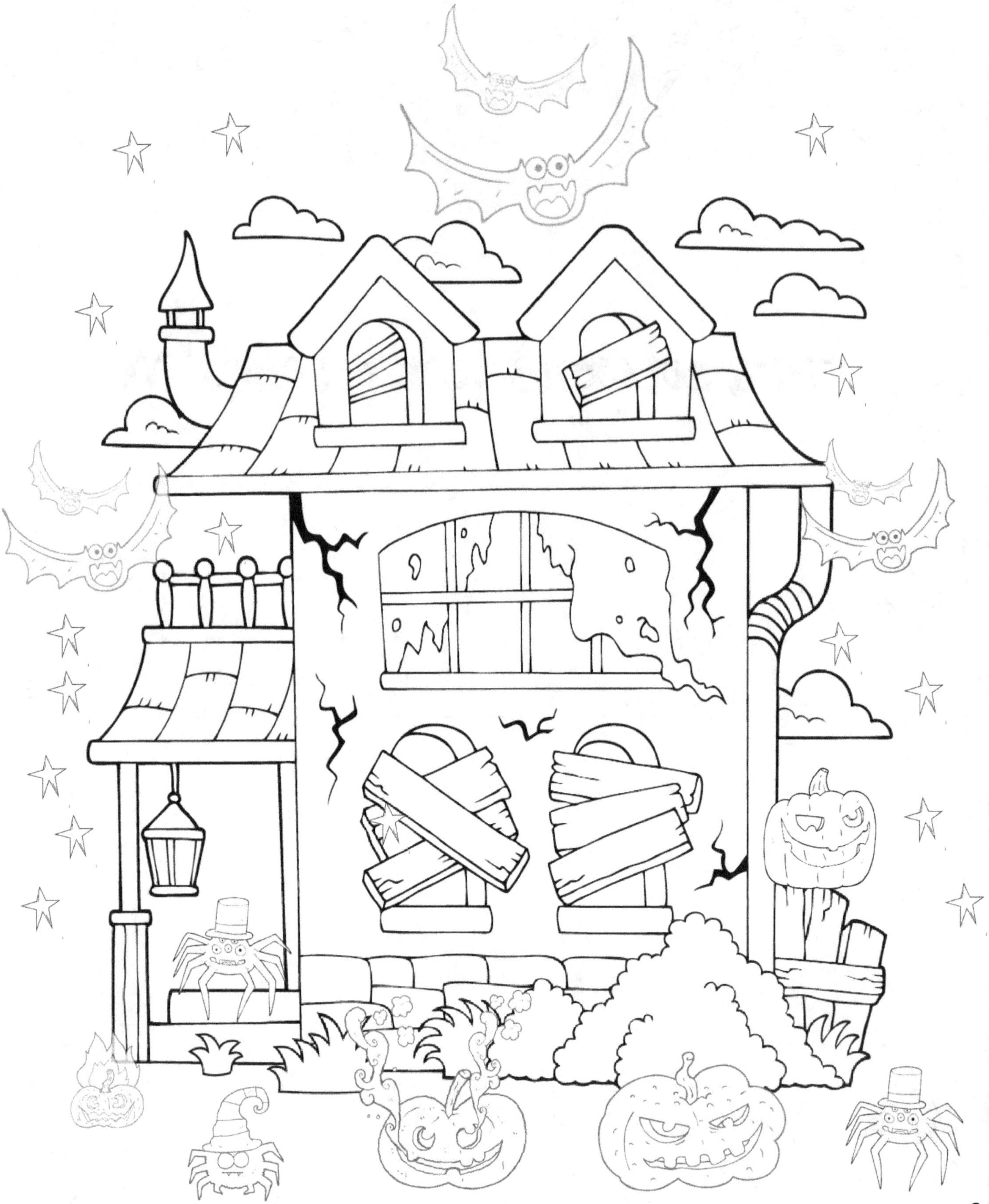

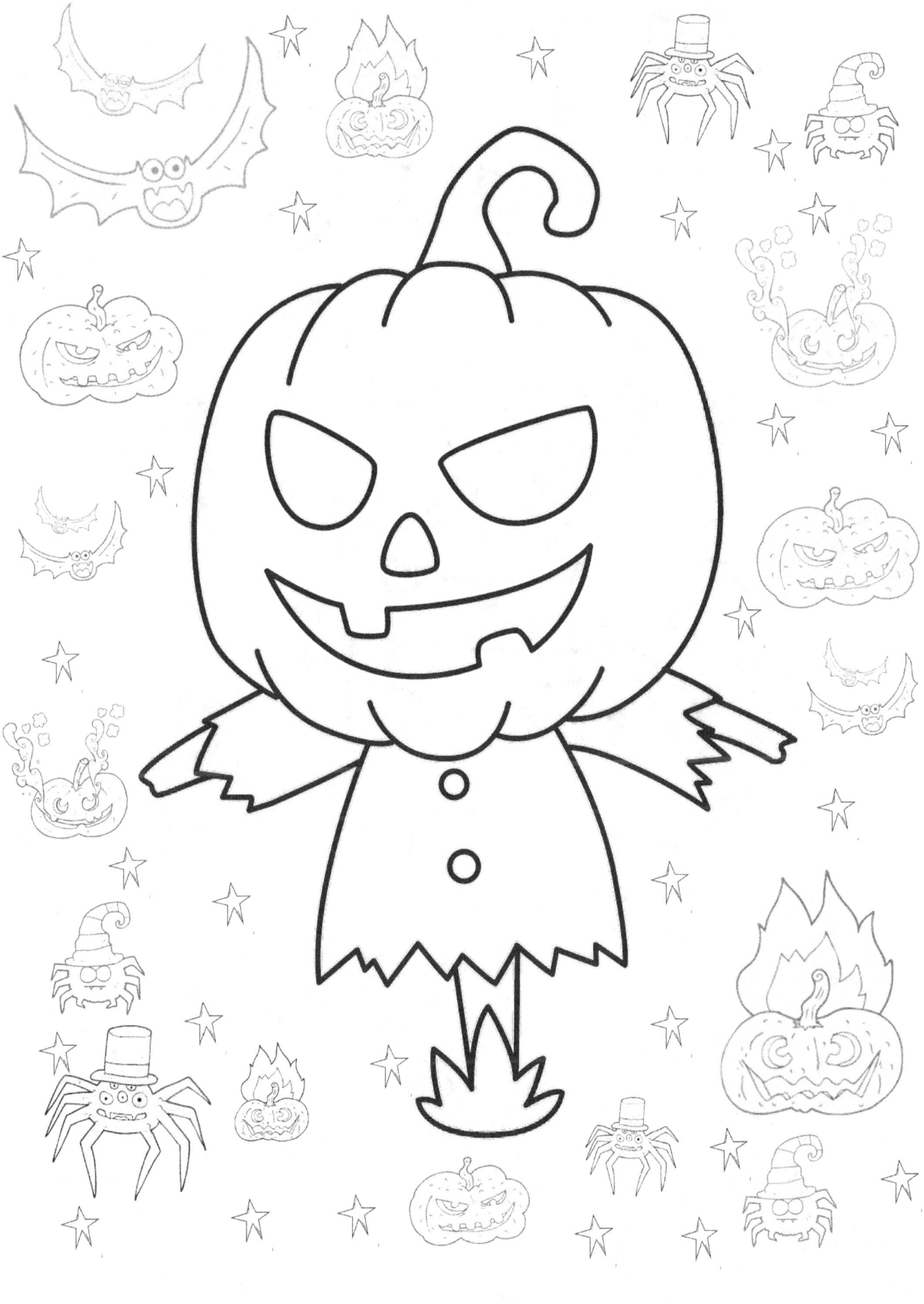

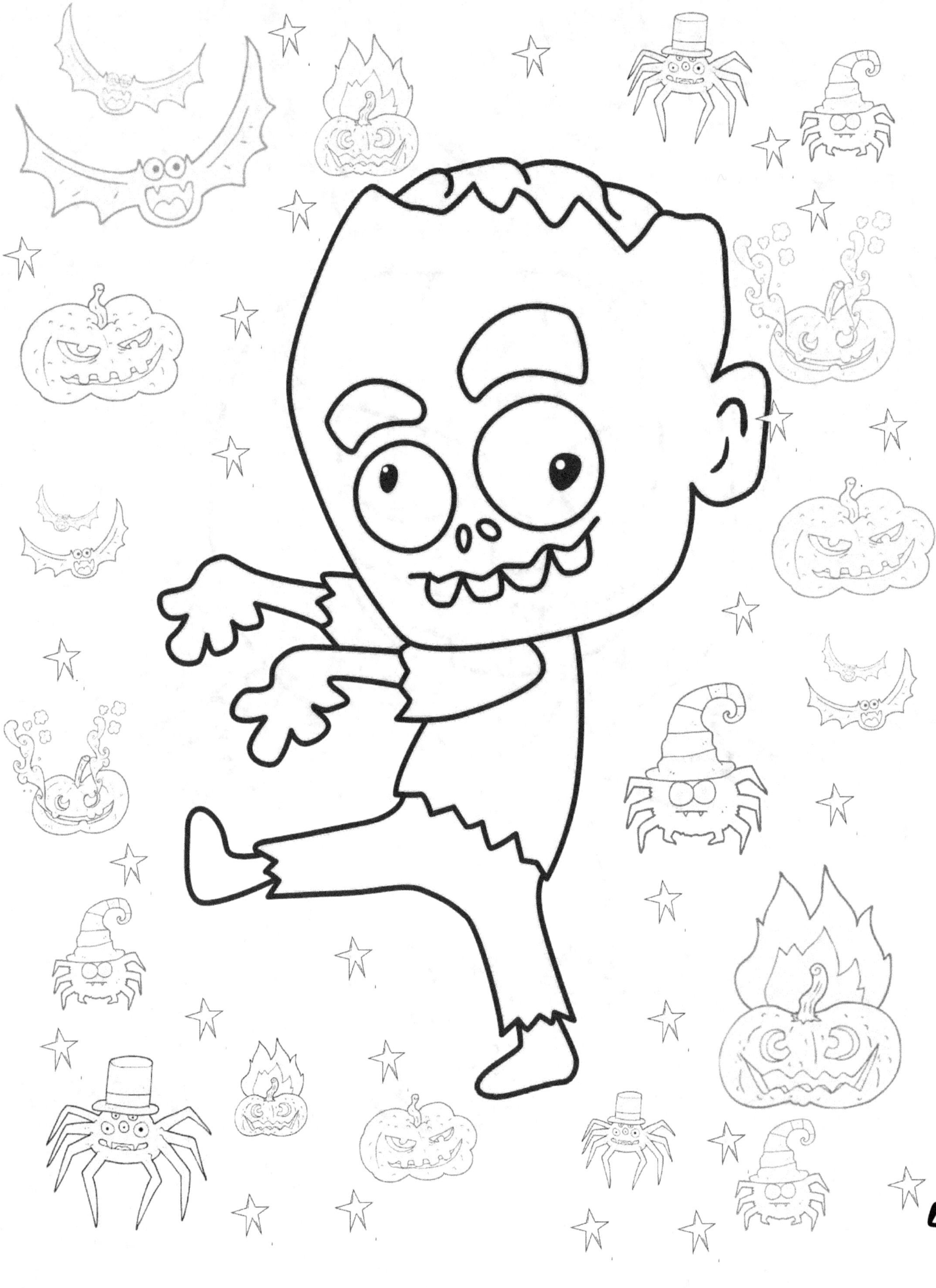

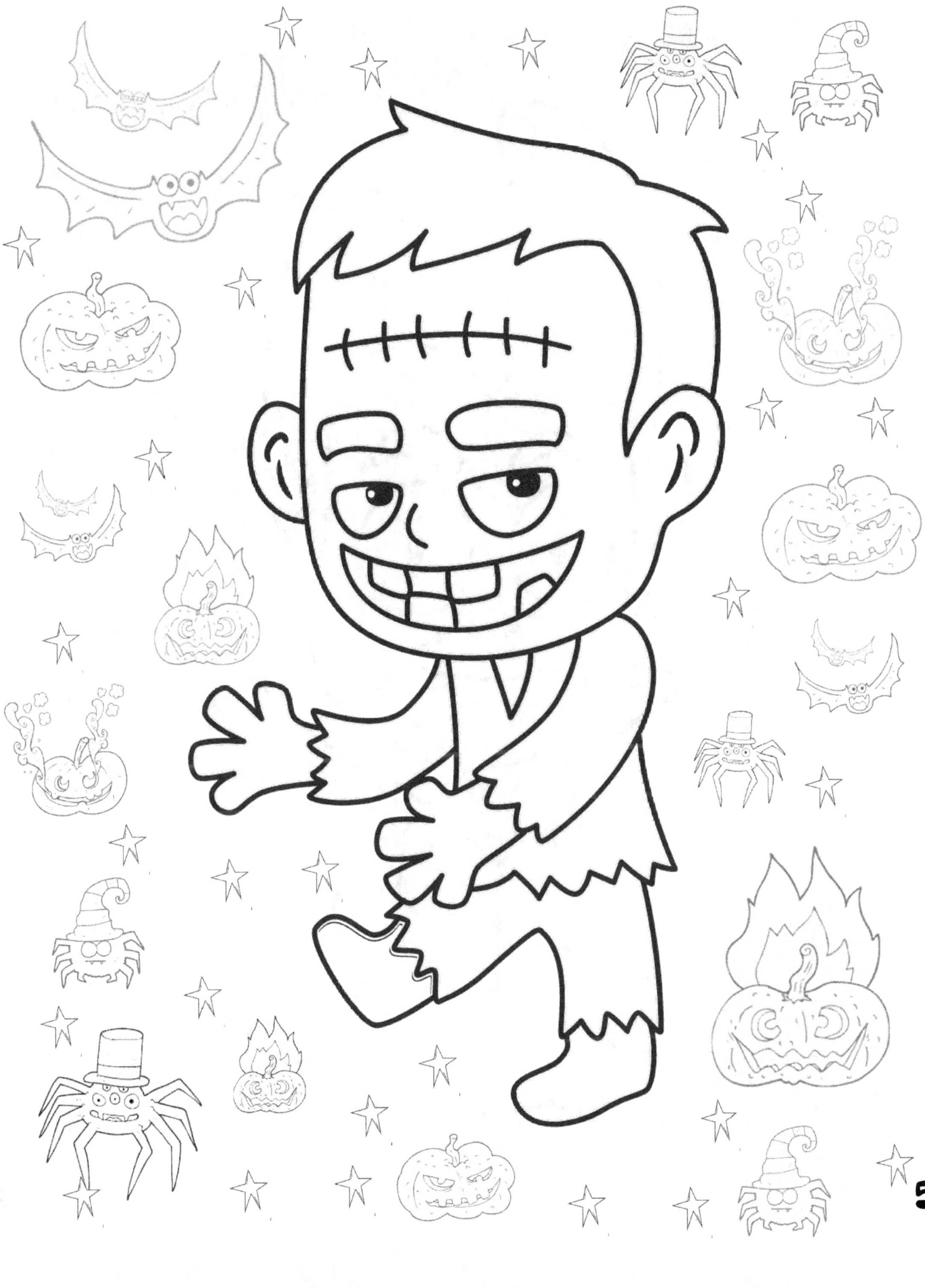

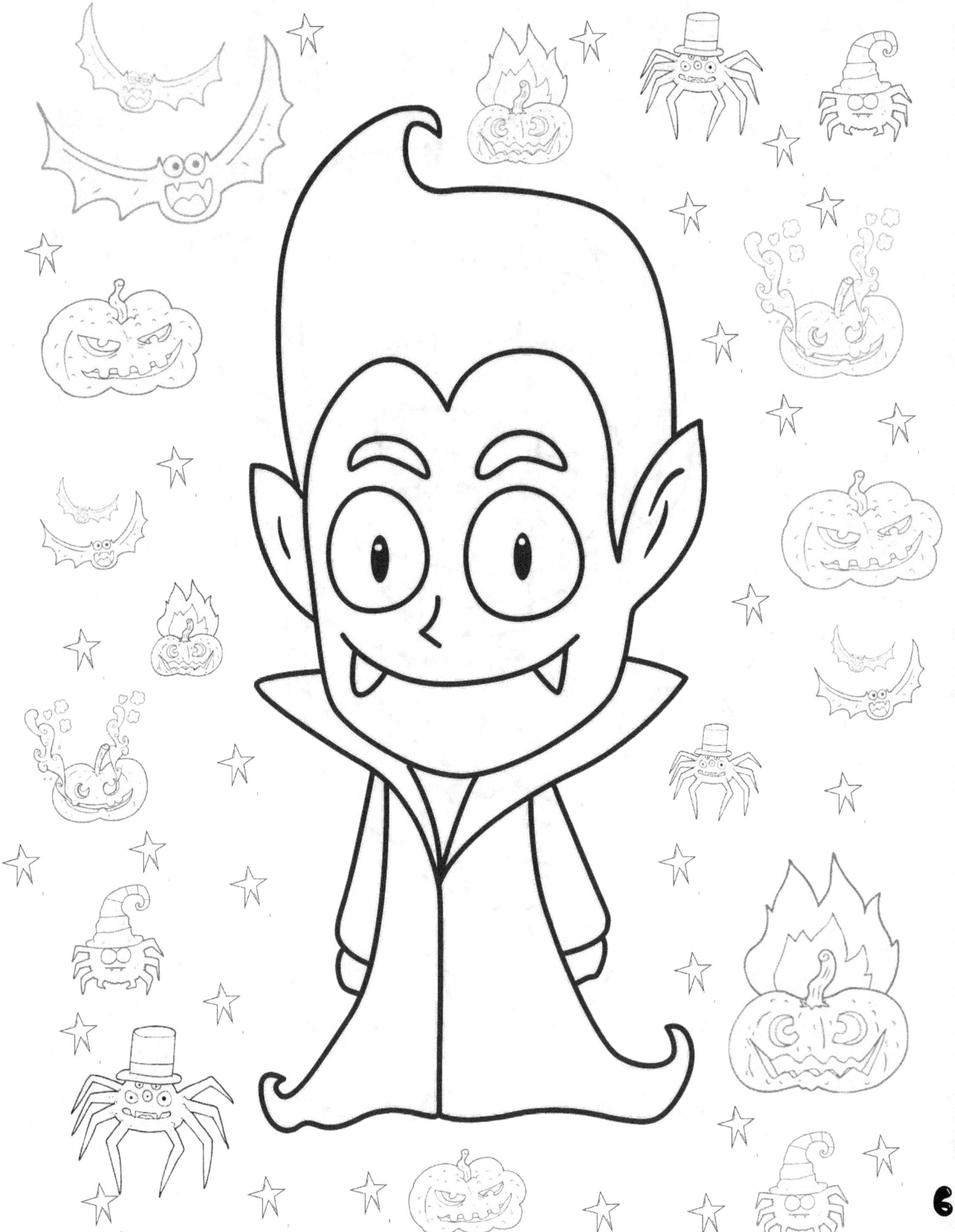

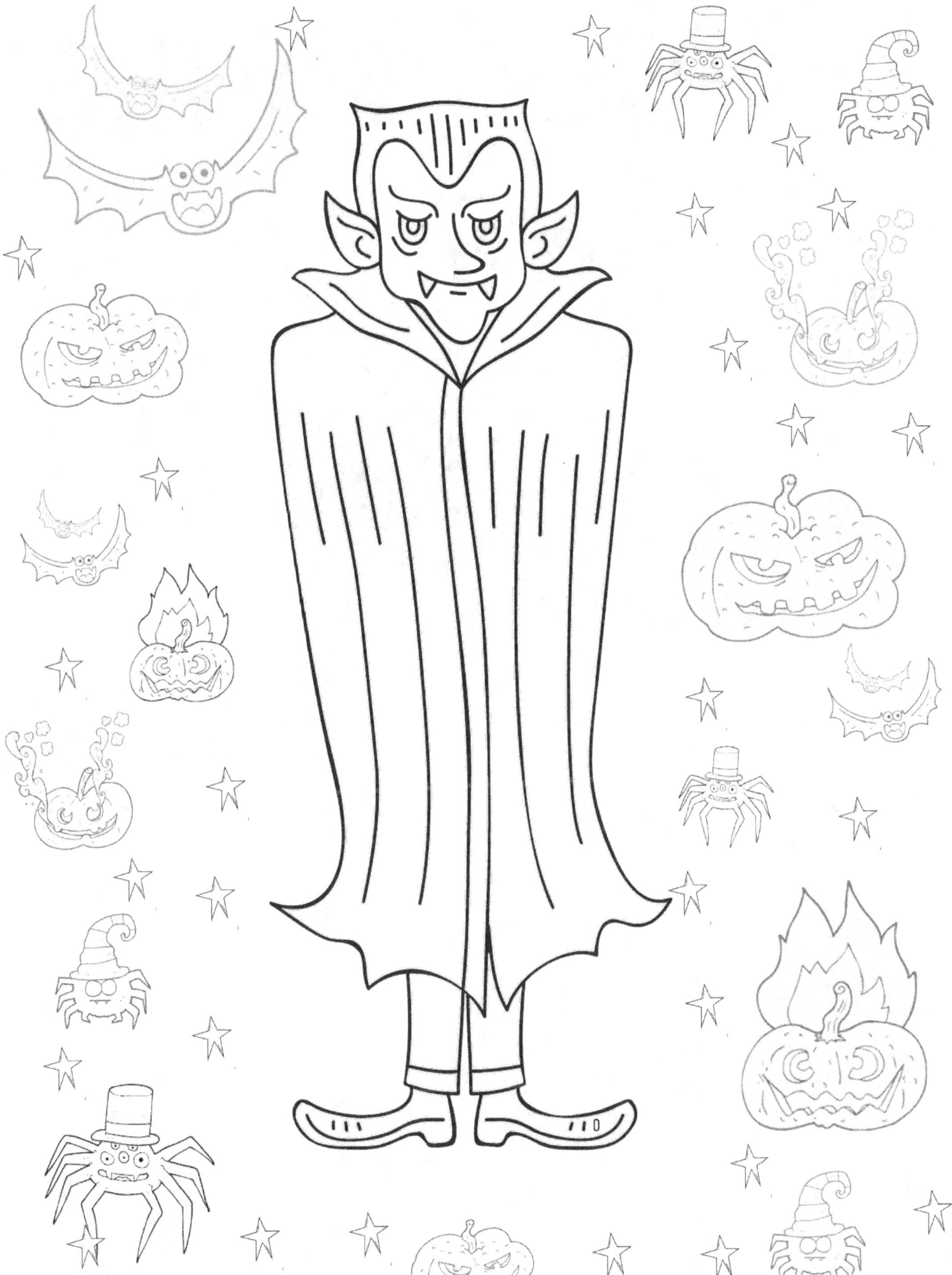

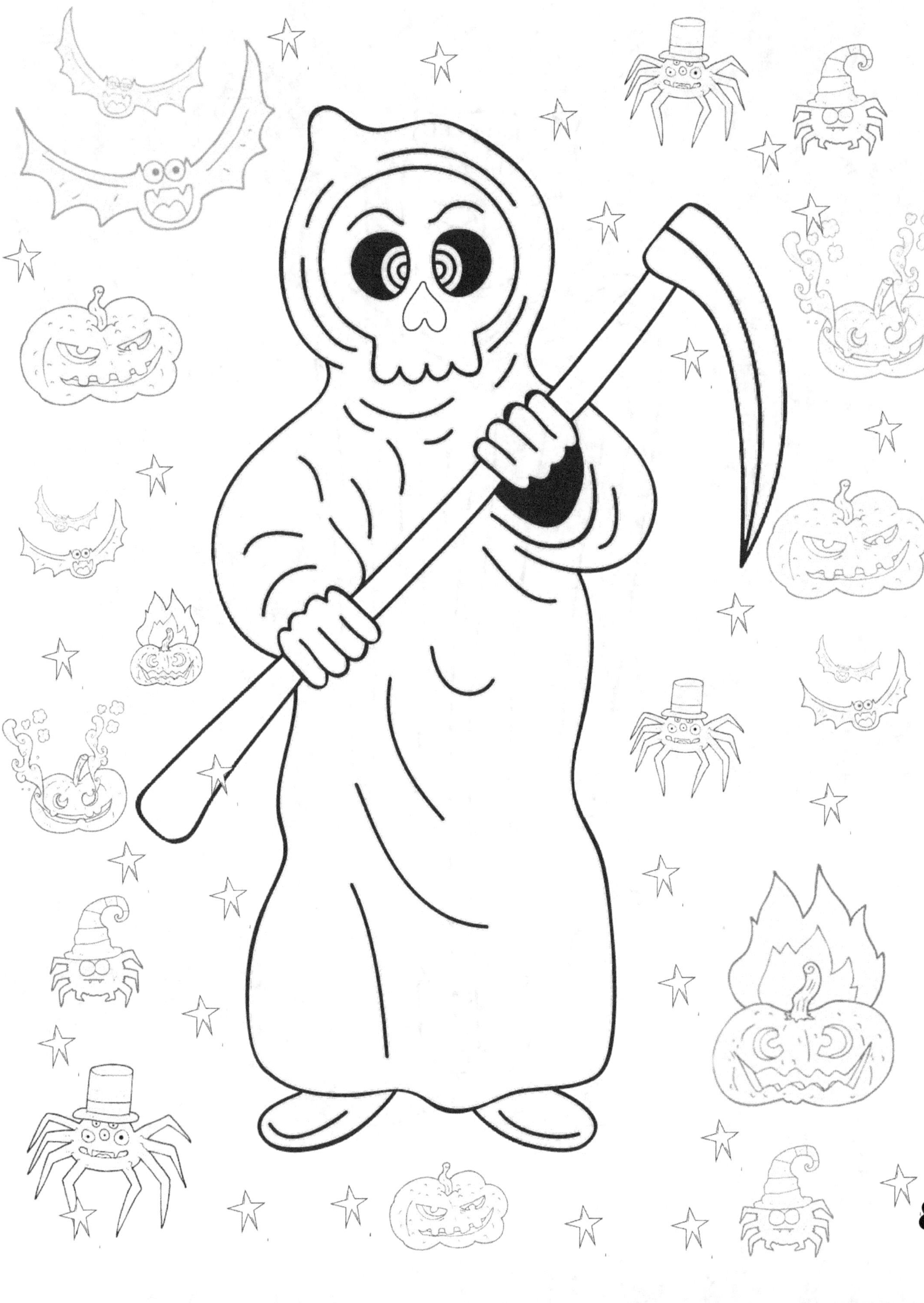

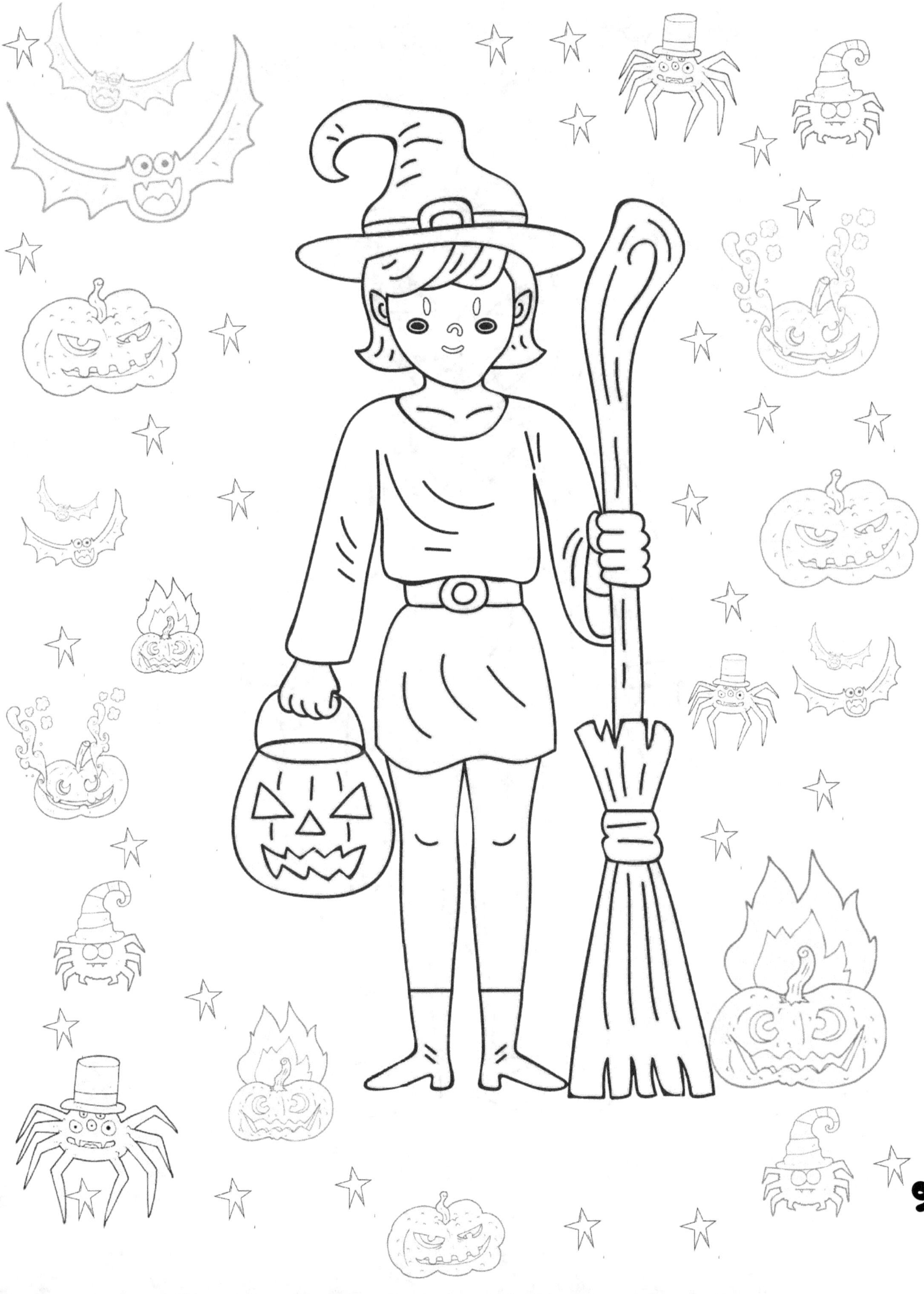

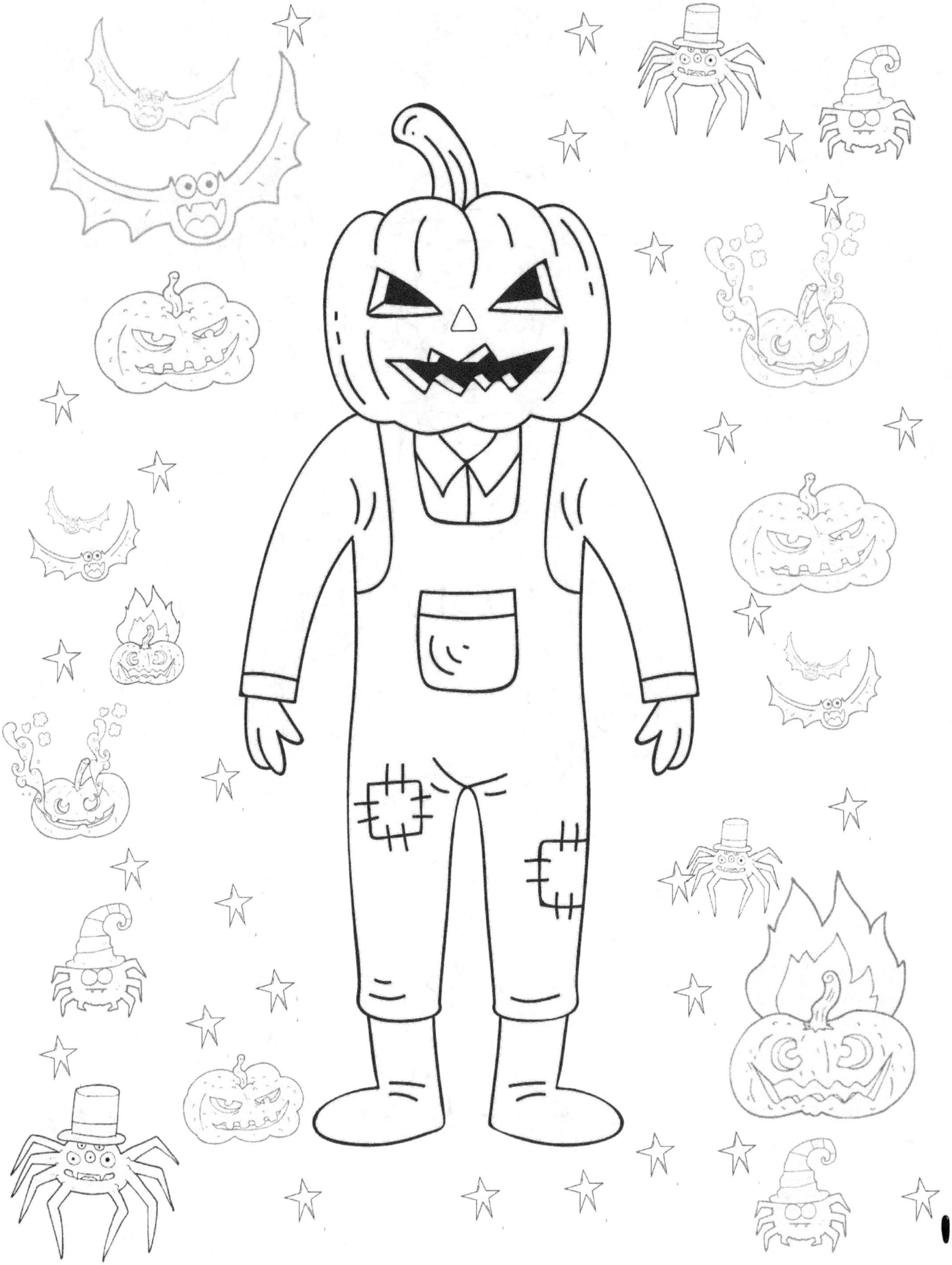

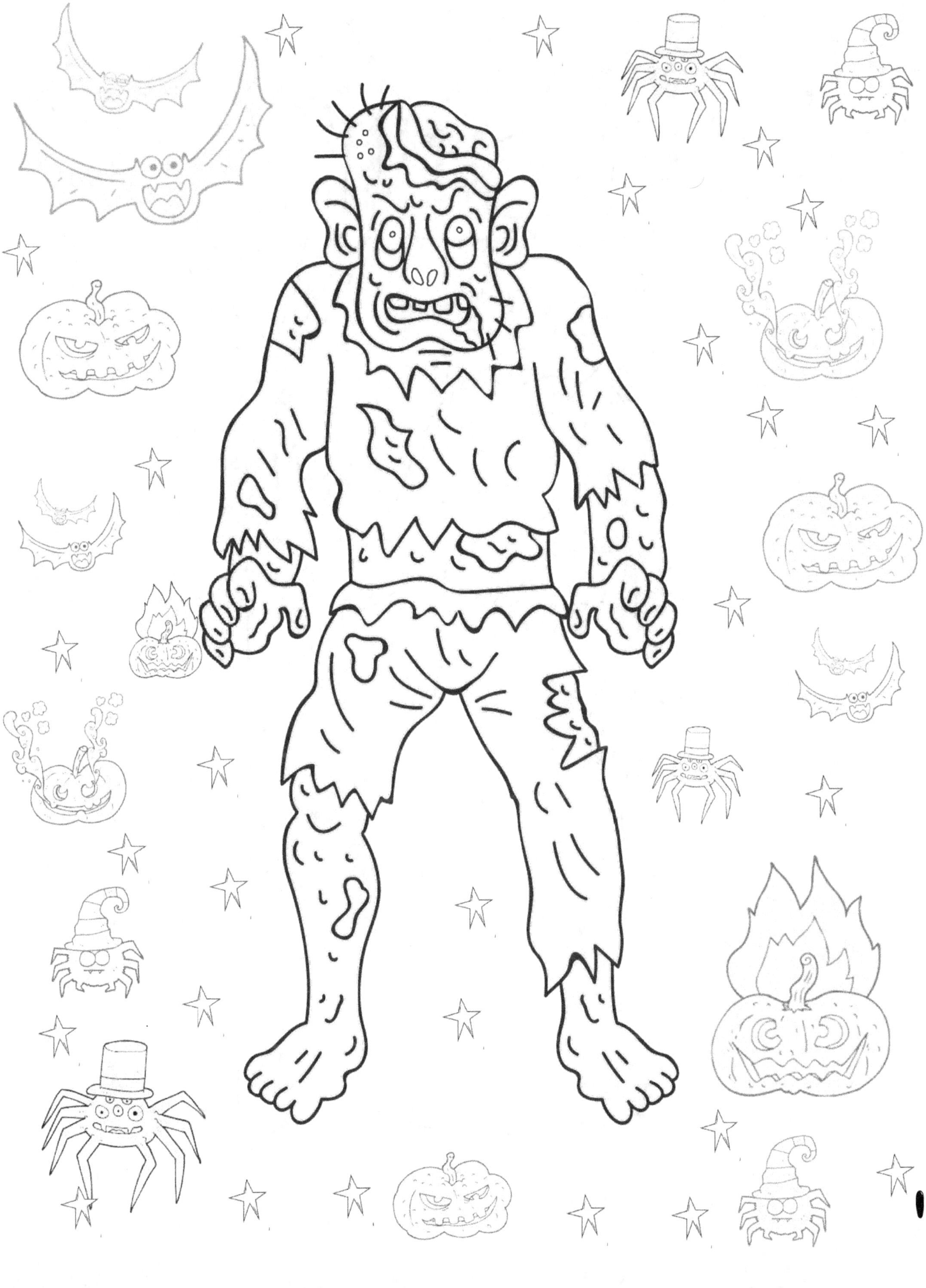

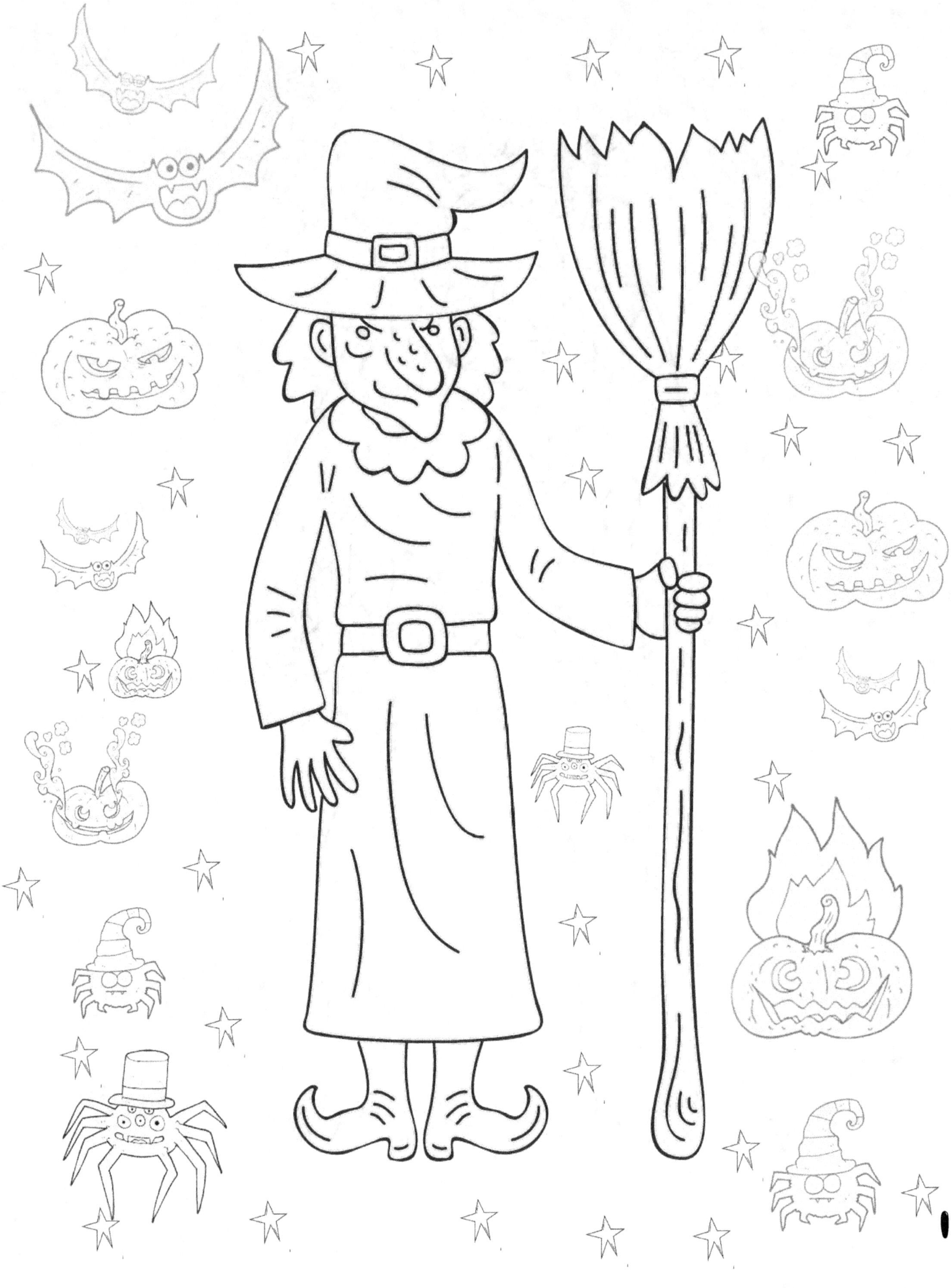

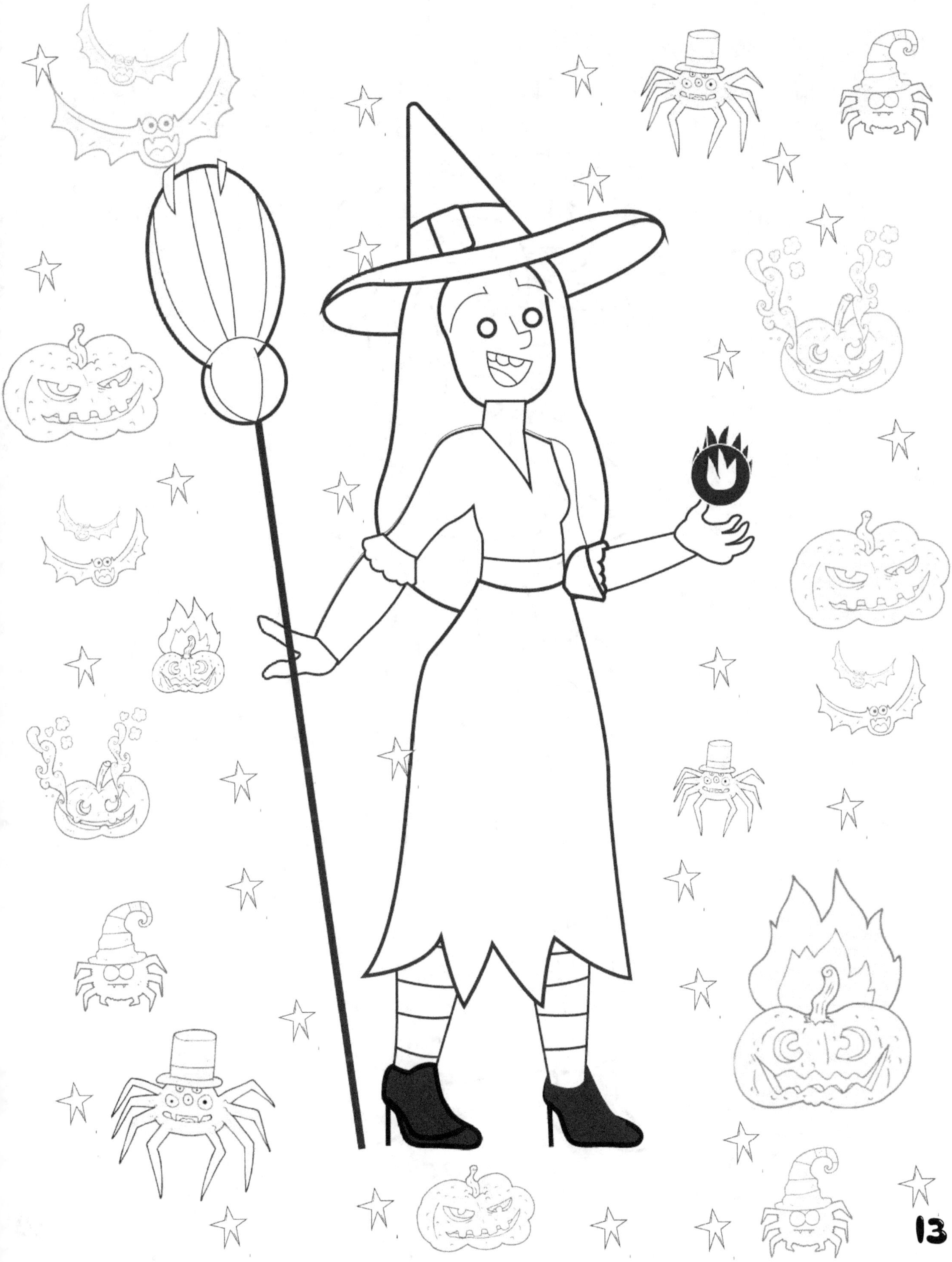

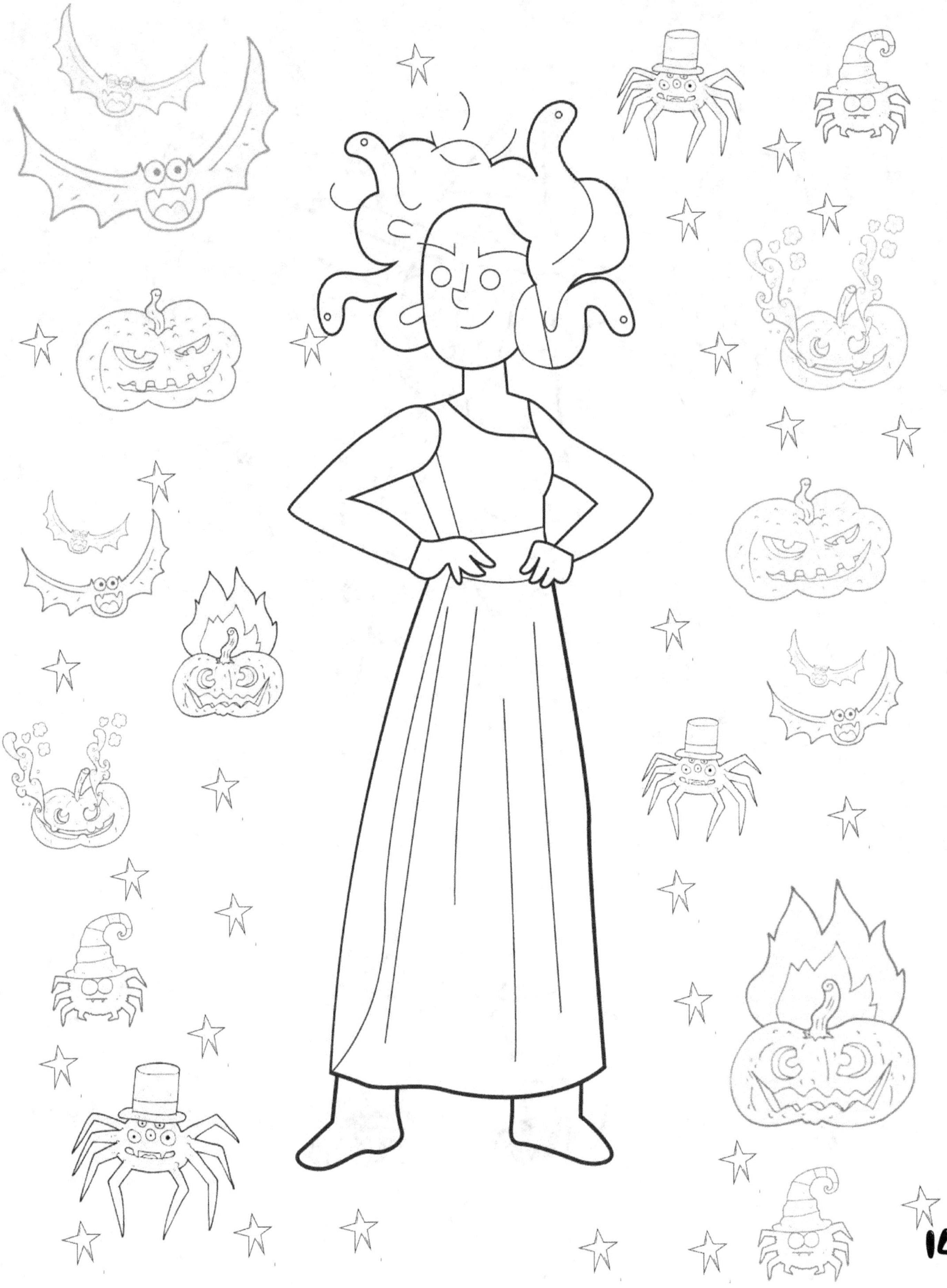

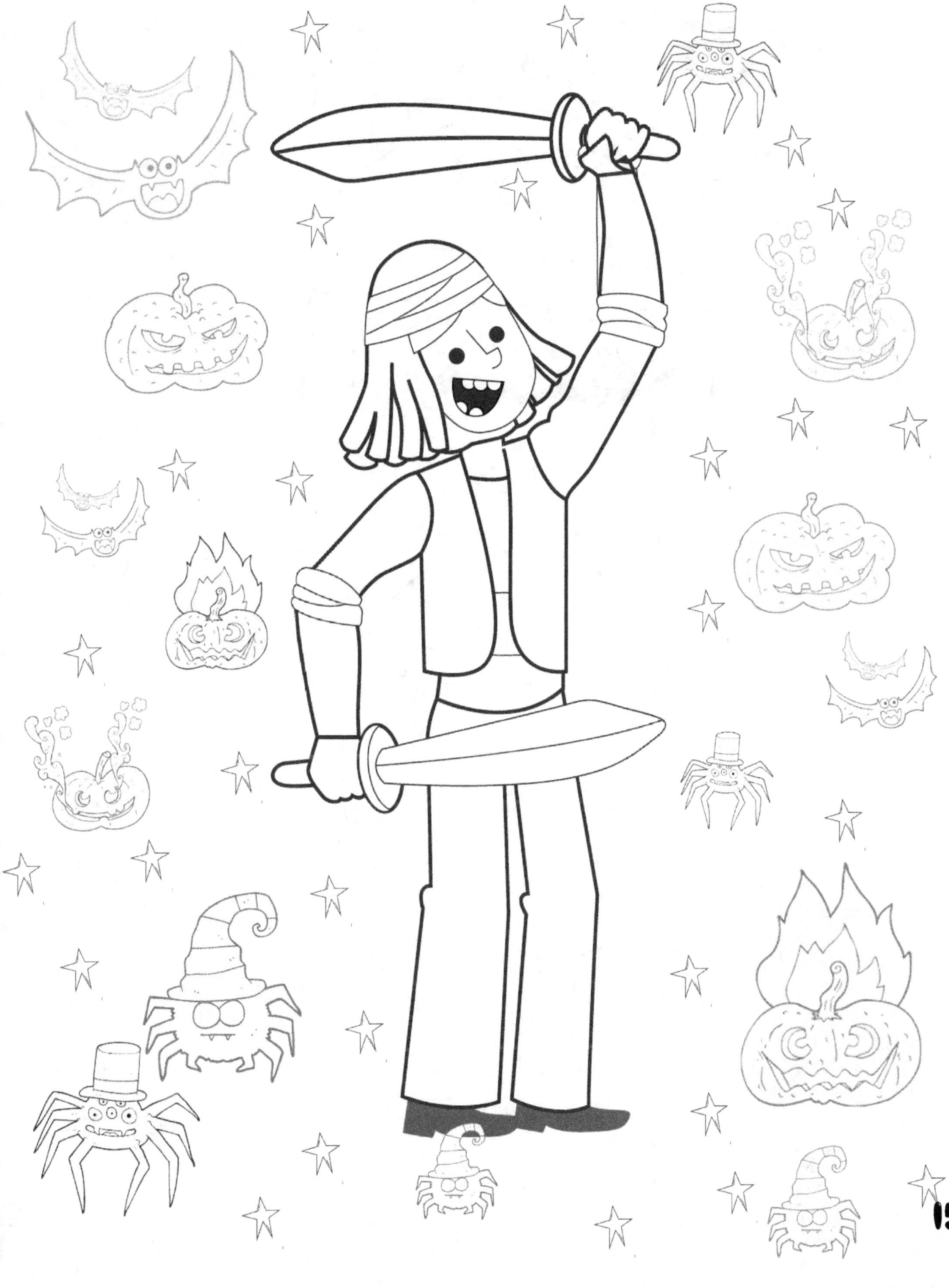

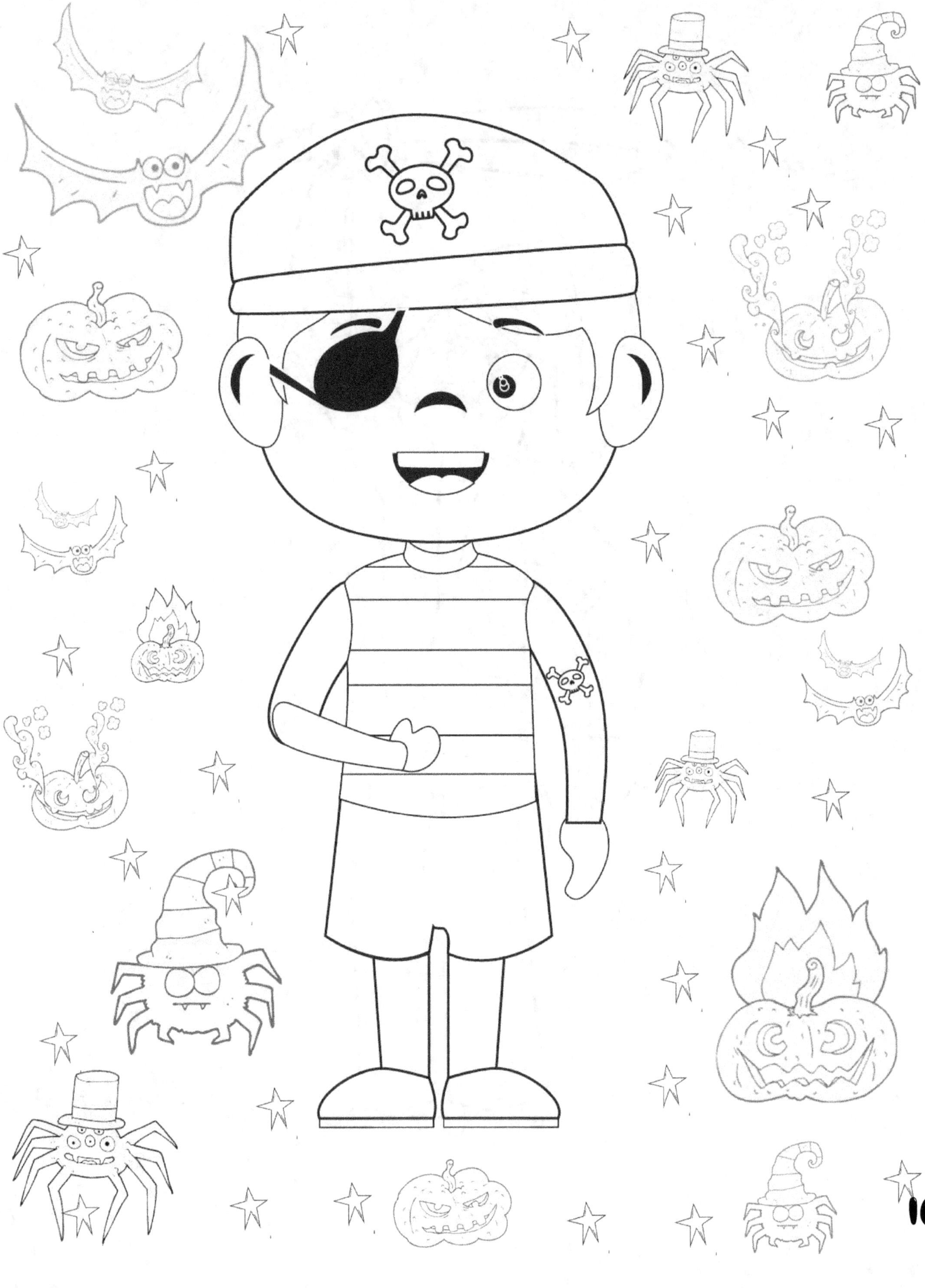

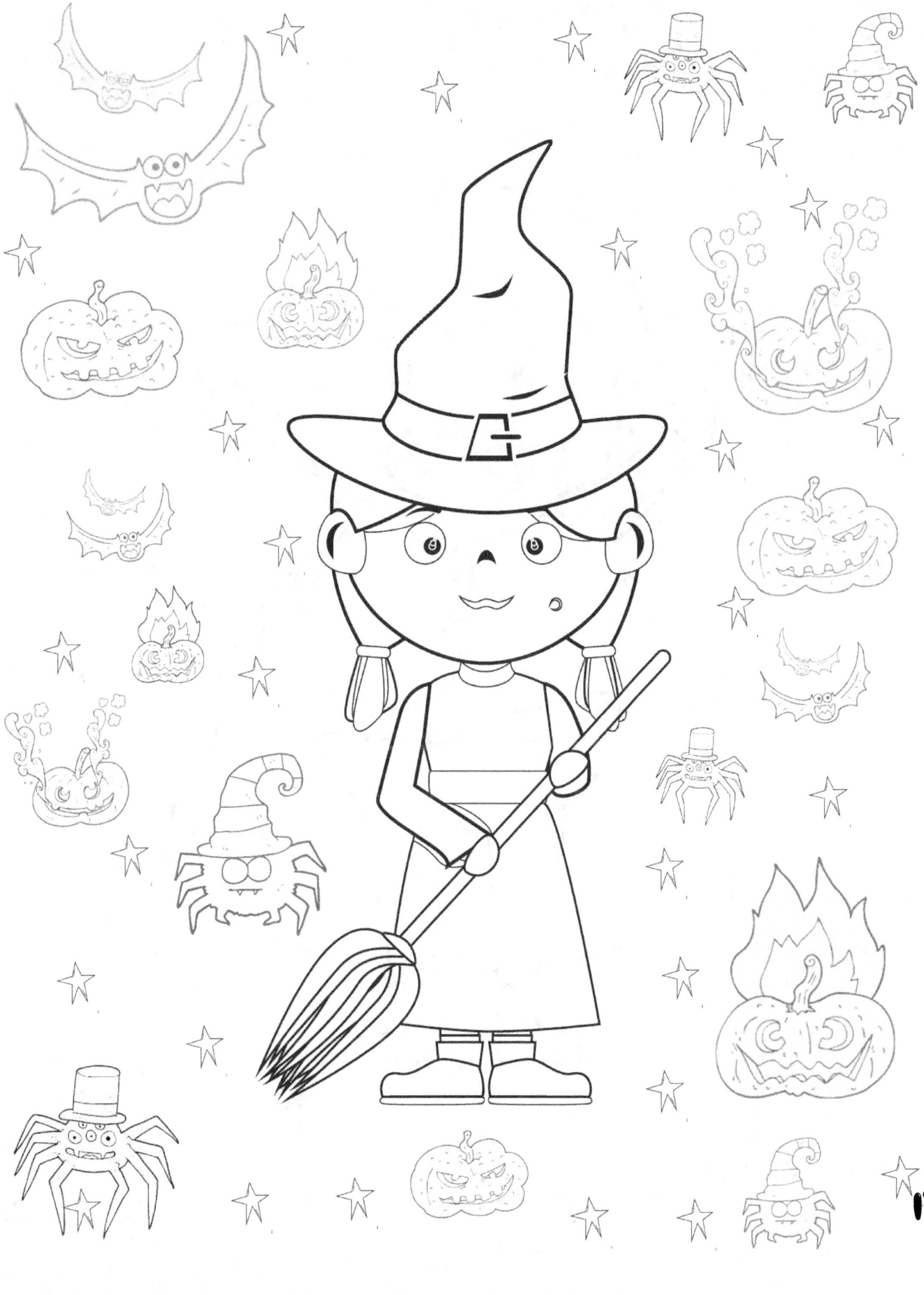

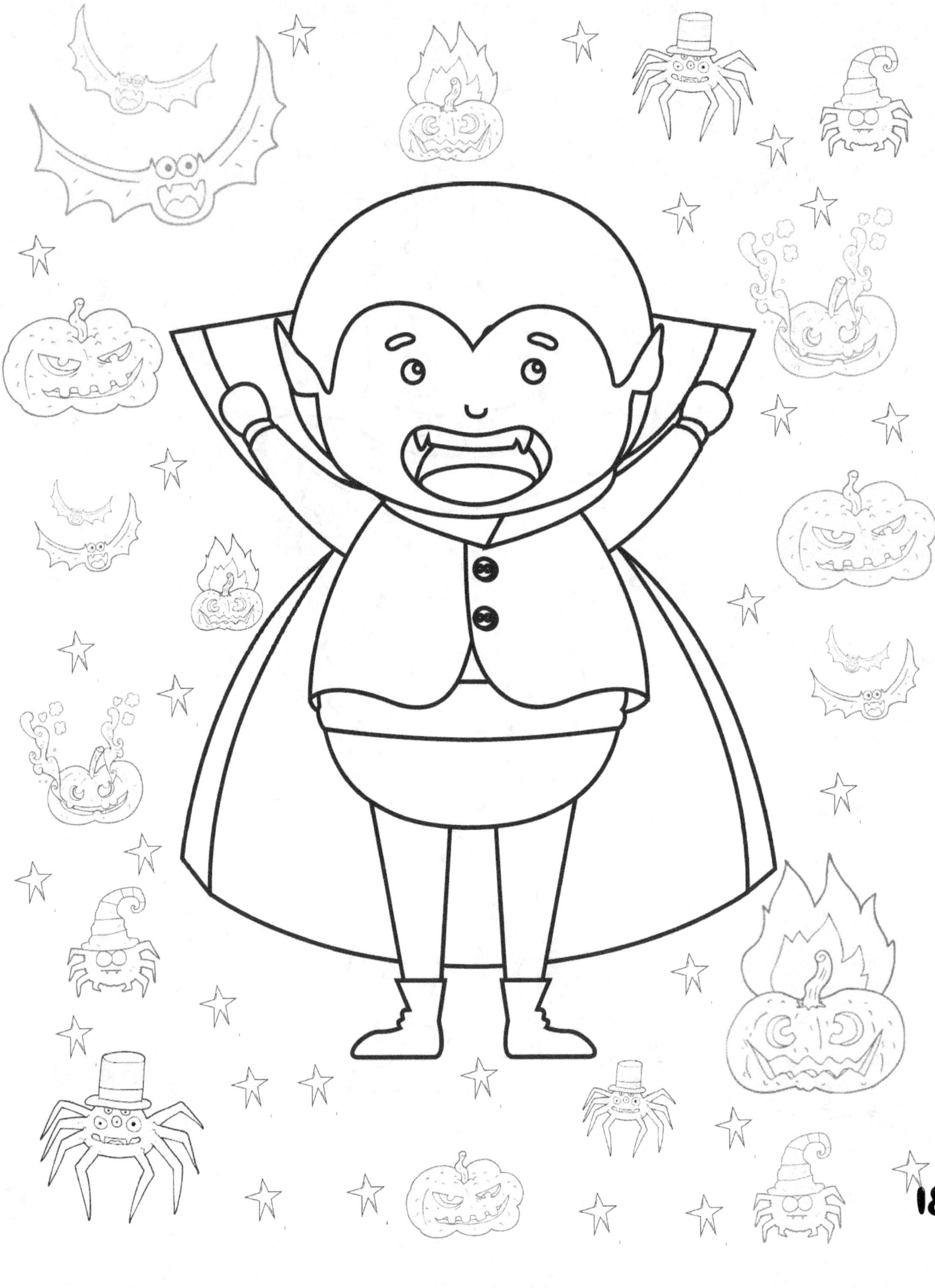

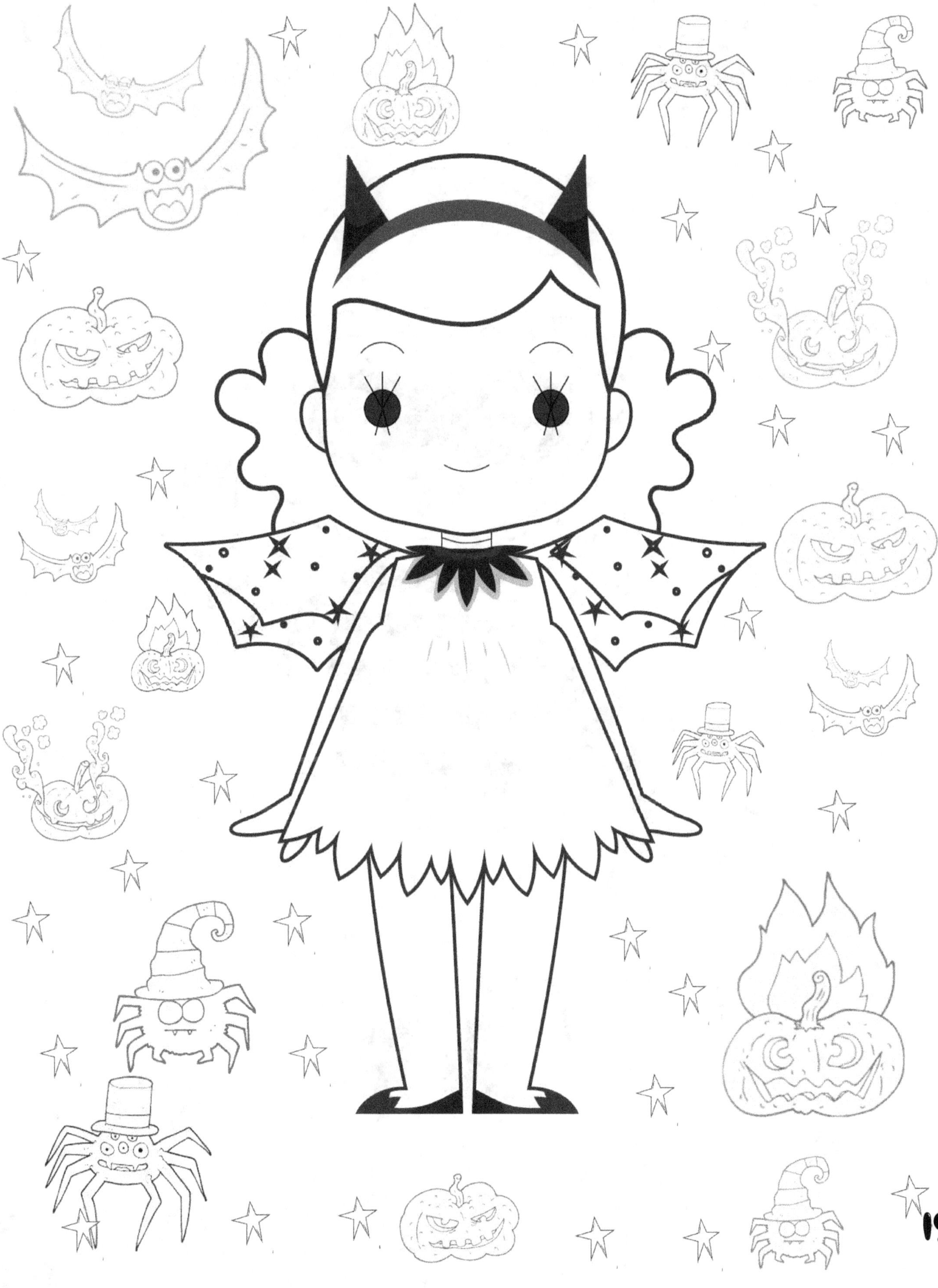

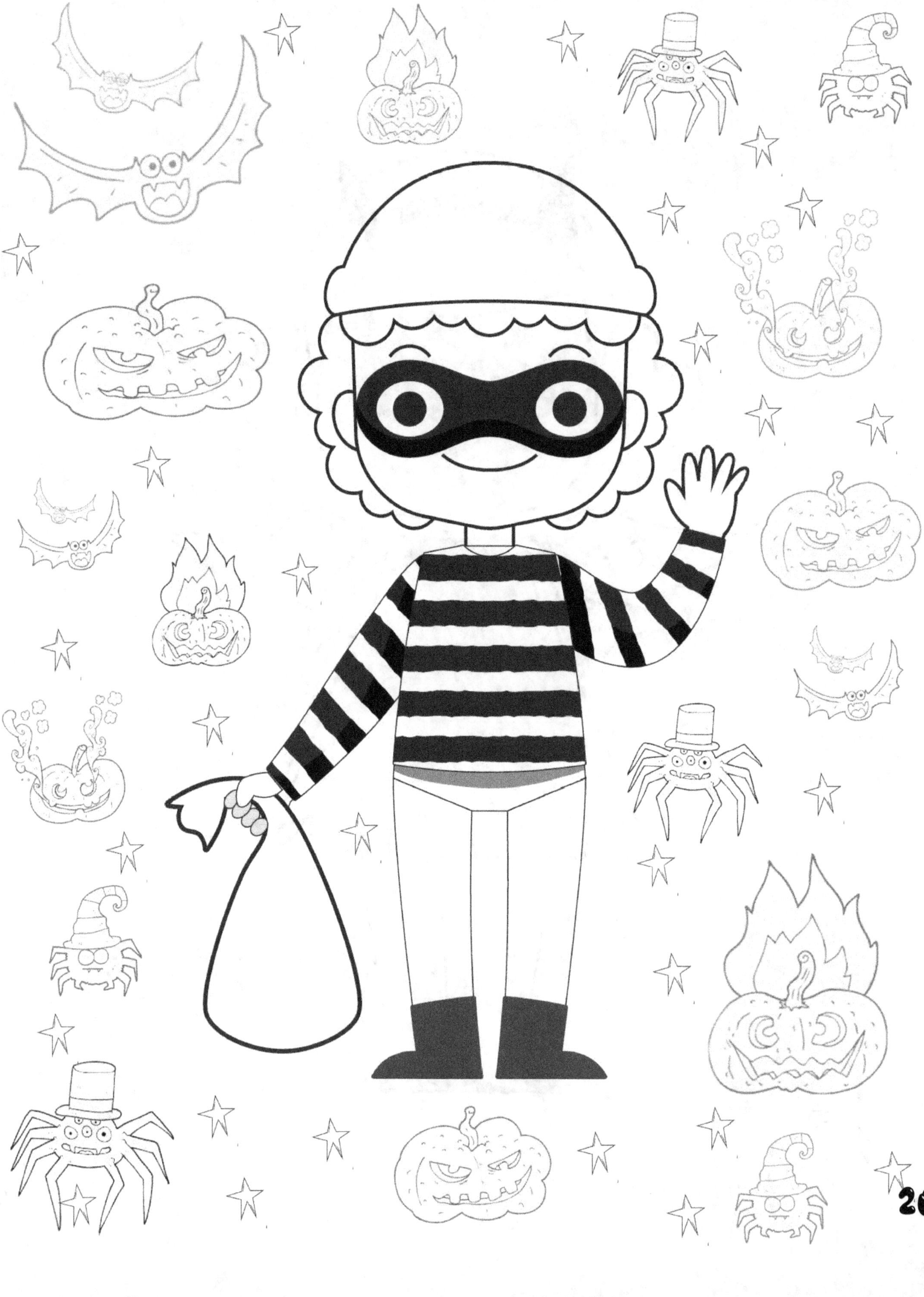

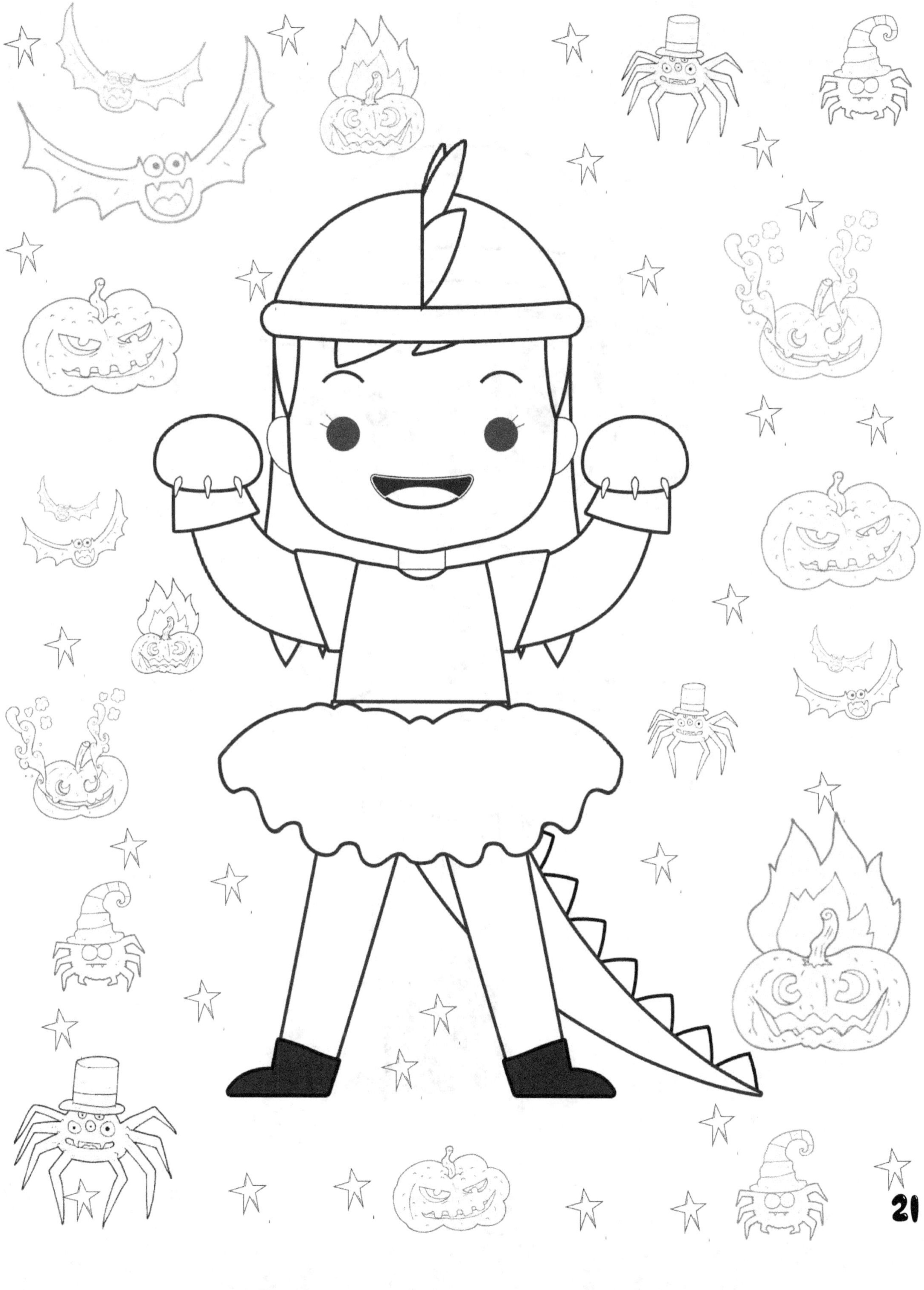

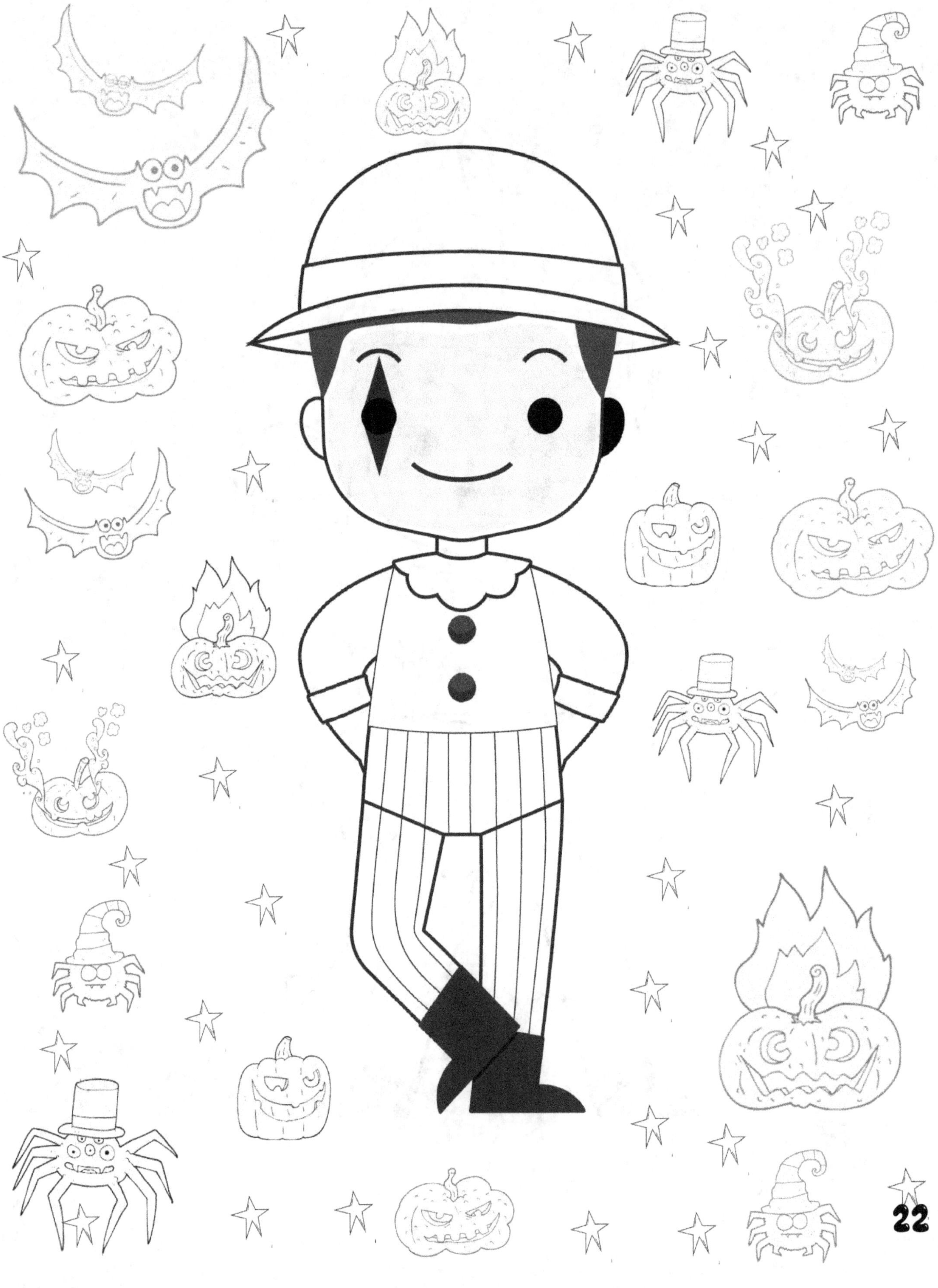

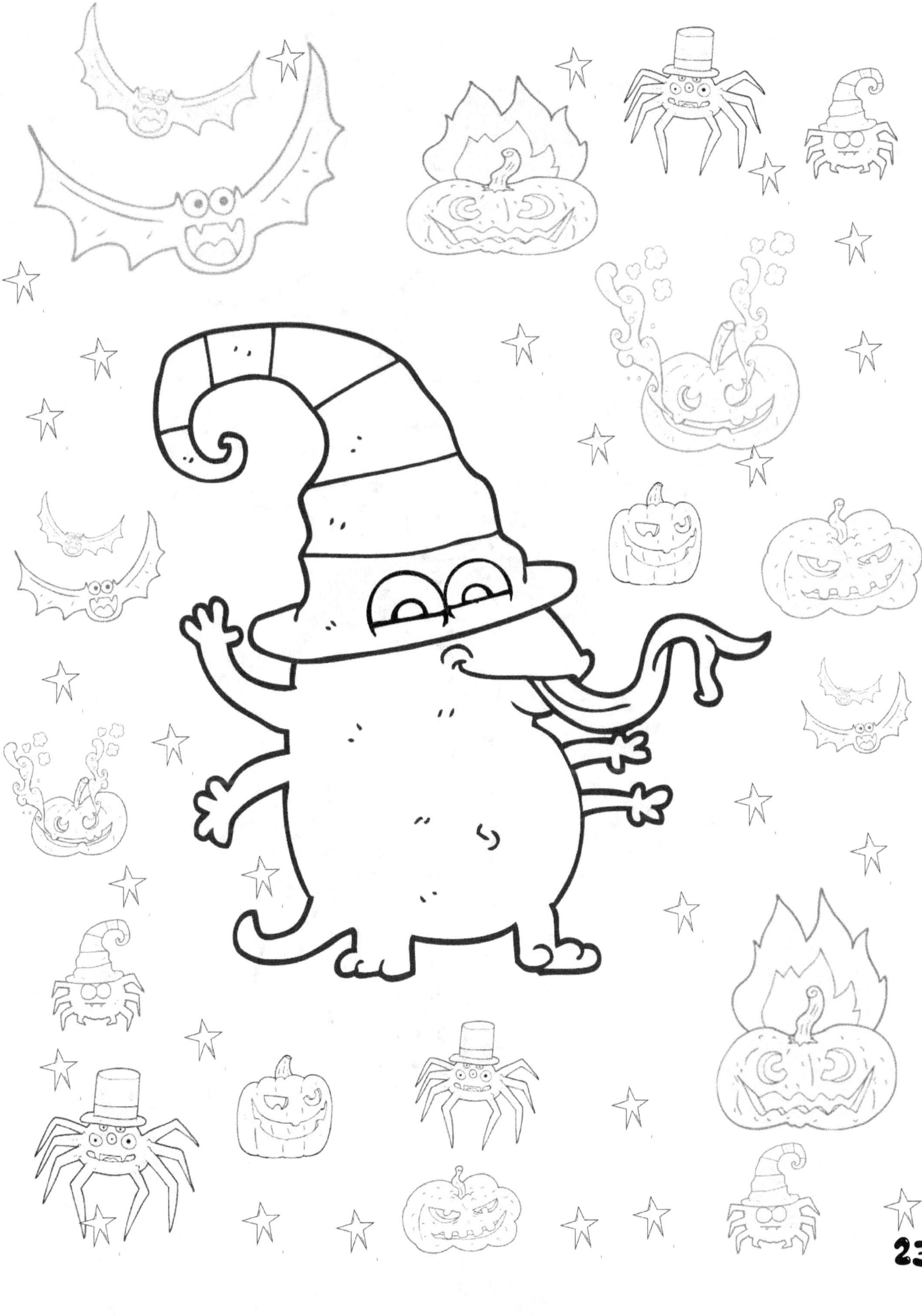

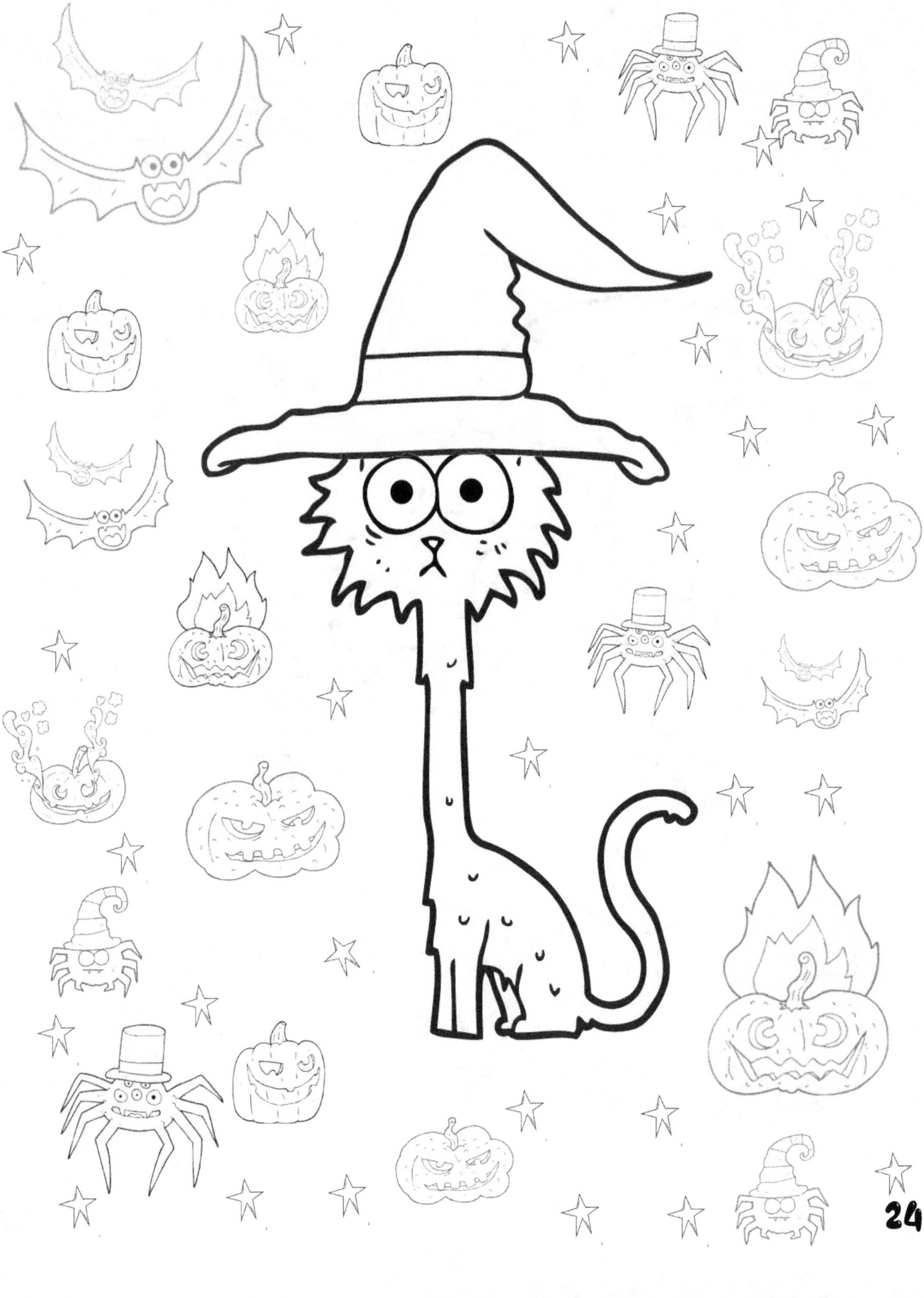

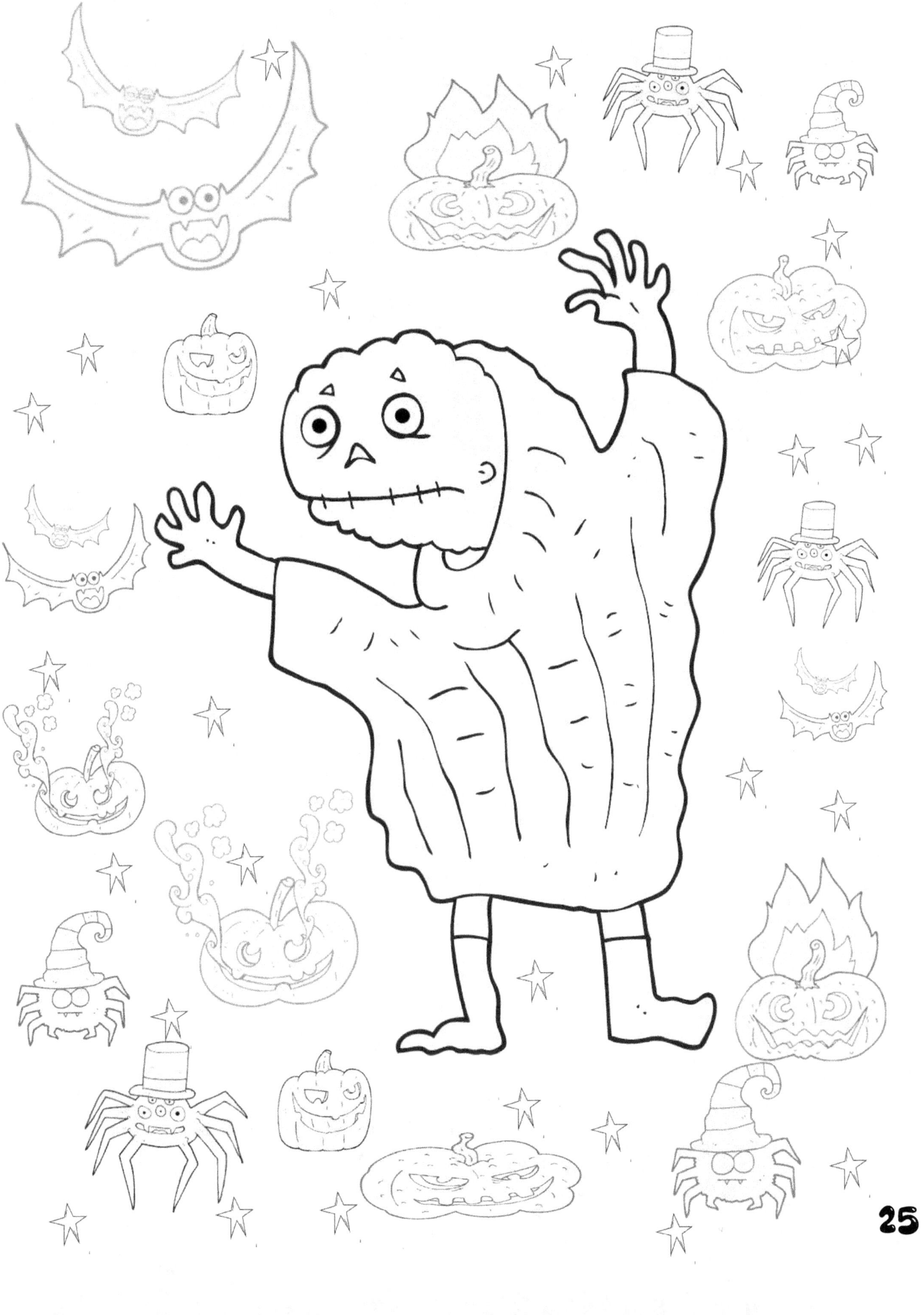

www.ingramcontent.com/pod-product-compliance
Lightning Source LLC
Chambersburg PA
CBHW080630220526
45467CB00011B/3457